John Fitzgerald Kennedy
CROSSWORD PUZZLES

The legacy of John "Jack" F. Kennedy lives on even though he was tragically killed just two years into his first term as president. At age 43, Kennedy brought youth, vitality, and optimism into the White House at a time when the country needed a change. He also brought his wife, the former Jacqueline "Jackie" Bouvier, a woman of grace and poise. She restored the White House to the glory it deserved and became an icon for many around the world.

The president's ancestors worked their way up the corporate and political ladder, rising above the discrimination of being Irish and Catholic to become business magnates and political powerhouses. As triumphant as the family story is, however, it is also marked with tragedy — assassinations, war deaths, medical conditions, scandals, and more. Despite these events, the Kennedys never strayed into the shadows.

The nation's 35th president went to Harvard, saw action in World War II, and served in various political jobs before seeking the highest office in the land. Kennedy had great plans for the country, envisioning an America free from racism and poverty, an America that could boast the best schools and economy in the world. His legacy was such that even though he died young, many programs he championed gained steam after his death.

An event that nearly led to nuclear war and catastrophic casualties defined Kennedy's administration. Against the backdrop of the Cold War and the partitioning of Berlin in Germany, the Bay of Pigs invasion of Cuba, and new ties between Fidel Castro and Soviet leaders, the Cuban Missile Crisis brought the world to the brink of war. It was largely because of Kennedy's grace under fire that the United States avoided battle with the Soviet Union.

Kennedy also dreamed of Americans landing on the moon, and sought to finance several space programs to realize this dream by the end of the 1960s. Though he died before Neil Armstrong stepped foot on the moon, it is in part because of Kennedy that Armstrong was able to make the giant leap for mankind.

Kennedy still captivates Americans for his eloquence in navigating the country through some of its most trying times. The words he used to lift a nation still echo clearly today. He asked not what his country could do for him, but what he could do for his country.

PUZZLE ANSWERS ON BACK PAGES

© Museum Masterworks 2010 ISBN: 978-0-9844156-7-0

All Rights Reserved. No part of this publication may be reproduced or transmitted in any form or by any means, electronic or mechanical, including photocopy, recording or any other information storage and retrieval system, without prior permission in writing from the publisher.

Before the Presidency

ACROSS

1. John F. Kennedy, nicknamed "Jack," was one of _____ children

8. Married Jacqueline Bouvier, a writer who was _____ years his junior

9. During World War II, a _____ warship rammed the PT-109, which he commanded. Stranded at sea, John F. Kennedy led his crew to an island, where they waited in hope of being rescued

12. Was the 1960 _____ nominee for president

15. Attended boarding school in this state

17. After brother Joe died in battle and World War II ended, John F. Kennedy entered politics, running for _____ in 1946

19. Went to this Ivy League university, where he injured his spine while playing football

DOWN

2. John F. Kennedy's father was appointed United States ambassador to this country in 1937, which fueled the son's interest in international affairs

3. Awarded the Navy and _____ Corps Medal for his efforts in World War II

4. The Kennedy summer home is in Hyannis Port on _____ Cod

5. The Kennedys practice the _____ faith

JOHN F. KENNEDY PRESIDENTIAL LIBRARY & MUSEUM, BOSTON

6. John F. Kennedy and his big brother Joe joined this military branch during World War II

7. Home state of the Kennedys

10. Had whooping cough, the measles, chicken pox, and _____ fever all before the age of three

11. Wrote "Profiles in Courage," a book about United States _____ who risked their careers for the things in which they believed, for which he won the Pulitzer Prize

13. Nickname of son John Jr.

14. His grandfather served as mayor of this city

16. John F. Kennedy's great-grandparents came from this country

18. First name of John F. Kennedy's mother

JOHN F. KENNEDY PRESIDENTIAL LIBRARY & MUSEUM, BOSTON

JOHN F. KENNEDY PRESIDENTIAL LIBRARY & MUSEUM, BOSTON

The Kennedy Dynasty

ACROSS

2. President Kennedy's grandfather, John F. Fitzgerald, was nicknamed "_____ Fitz"

6. Brothers Robert and Edward Kennedy both attended law school at the University of _____

11. President Bill Clinton nominated youngest sister Jean Kennedy ambassador to _____ in 1993. She was influential in that country's peace process

12. Sister Kathleen Kennedy volunteered for the Red _____ during World War II. Her husband was killed during the war

13. The Kennedy family had a private audience with the new _____, Pius XII, in 1939. Rose was granted the rare title of papal countess in 1951 for her exemplary motherhood and charitable works

14. Brother Robert and his wife Ethel had _____ children

16. Oldest brother Joe, Jr. died in a World War II plane explosion near the _____ Channel

17. Joseph Kennedy, father of President Kennedy, was a prominent banker before moving to the _____ industry and becoming the head of several production companies

DOWN

1. After _____ ended, father Joseph Kennedy established an alcohol importation company. He was later appointed chairman of the new Securities and Exchange Commission, and served

as a United States ambassador

3. The Special _____ began with sister Eunice Kennedy Shriver, who started a camp in her backyard for intellectually disabled children and adults

4. Family matriarch Rose was very active in her children's lives. She, along with her daughters, played hostess to many parties thrown to support John F. Kennedy's race to the White House. These get-togethers were known as the Kennedy _____

5. Robert Kennedy led a campaign against _____ crime, exposing union organizers Jimmy Hoffa and David Beck

7. Youngest brother Edward Kennedy was elected United States senator from Massachusetts _____ times

8. Robert Kennedy was assassinated in 1968 while campaigning for _____

9. Mother Rose Kennedy stated that her biggest regret was not going to this all-girls college

10. Father Joseph Kennedy left the Republican Party and supported Franklin _____ in 1932

13. R. Sargent Shriver, husband of sister Eunice Kennedy, was instrumental in the creation of the _____ Corps, an international volunteer organization

15. Youngest brother Edward "Ted" Kennedy was known as the "_____ of the Senate," and was instrumental in many legislative acts and reforms

WWII and John F. Kennedy

JOHN F. KENNEDY PRESIDENTIAL LIBRARY & MUSEUM, BOSTON

ACROSS

5. PT stands for _____ Torpedo

8. The PT-109 was struck by a Japanese destroyer during this month of 1943

12. Many sailors were sickened from inhaling _____ from the fuel

15. After joining the Navy at age 24, Ensign John F. Kennedy was first assigned to ONI, the Office of Naval _____, in Washington

16. When asked about being called a hero, John F. Kennedy said, "It was involuntary. They sank my _____"

17. After the impact, skipper John F. Kennedy ordered his men to _____ ship, in fear the PT boat would go up in flames

18. John F. Kennedy and his crew swam to an island, Plum Pudding, more than _____ miles away

DOWN

1. After coming in contact with natives, John F. Kennedy etched a message on the shell of this type of fruit, whose milk was the only nourishment the sailors had for days

2. _____ men apparently were killed in the ramming. Several jumped overboard

3. During the war, served in the South _____

4. Darkness and very low _____ made it difficult to see enemy ships

6. John F. Kennedy participated in PT boat training in this New England state (two words)

7. Received the _____ Heart for being injured in wartime

9. The men of PT-109 were finally _____, nearly a week after the incident

10. Engineer Patrick McMahon was severely injured and burned. Kennedy towed him for miles by the strap of a _____ (two words)

11. When John F. Kennedy realized a Japanese destroyer was approaching, he tried to turn the ship to _____, but was too late; PT-109 was rammed

13. The two servicemen who could not _____ were strapped to planks and carried through the water by the others

14. The Japanese navy's resupply convoy was known as the _____ Express

JOHN F. KENNEDY PRESIDENTIAL LIBRARY & MUSEUM, BOSTON

ABBIE ROWE, WHITE HOUSE/JOHN F. KENNEDY PRESIDENTIAL LIBRARY & MUSEUM, BOSTON

America During the Early 1960s

ACROSS

4. Wilt Chamberlain scored 100 points in a single _____ game, setting an NBA record

5. In August 1963, Arthur Ashe became the first _____ American to make the United States Davis Cup tennis team

7. West Coast state that played host to the 1960 Winter Olympics

8. "Who's Afraid of _____ Woolf" won the Tony Award for best play in 1963

9. On July 4, 1960, the first _____-star United States flag was flown

10. The first _____ Bond movie, "Dr. No," premiered in May 1963

12. "It's Now or Never" and "Are You Lonesome Tonight" by Elvis _____ topped the pop music charts in 1960

14. In June 1962, the _____ Court ruled that compulsory school prayer was unconstitutional

16. New York's Idlewild Airport became John F. Kennedy _____ Airport weeks after the president's death

17. JFK appointed NAACP attorney Thurgood _____ to the United States Court of Appeals in September 1961; he was later appointed to the U.S. Supreme Court in 1967

18. Johnny Carson began his long run as host of "The _____ Show" in October 1962

19. On September 28, 1960, Boston Red Sox slugger Ted _____ hit a homerun, one of many, before retiring from the game of baseball

20. Bob Dylan hit the music scene in 1961 at Folk City in _____ Village in New York City

DOWN

1. In September 1960, Cassius Clay, better known as _____ Ali, won the Olympic gold medal for boxing

2. "West Side _____" won the 1962 Academy Award for best motion picture

3. Author Ernest _____ and baseball legend Ty Cobb died in July 1961

6. The first live telecast of a presidential news _____ occurred on January 25, 1961

10. ABC's first color television show, which premiered in 1962, was "The _____," a cartoon about a futuristic family

11. The Reverend Martin Luther King Jr. was arrested in this Georgia city during a mass sit-in in October 1960

13. The _____, a popular British rock band, invaded the United States in 1964

15. Harper Lee won the _____ Prize for her novel "To Kill a Mockingbird" in 1961

The 35th President of the United States

ACROSS

1. The _____ wage was increased — from $1 to $1.15 an hour — and expanded during John F. Kennedy's presidency

4. Sending out a warning to other countries opposed to democracy, President Kennedy asserted, "Let every nation know, whether it wishes us well or ill, that we shall pay any price, bear any burden, meet any hardship, support any friend, oppose any foe to assure the survival and success of _____"

5. Upon becoming president, John F. Kennedy stated, "Let the word go forth from this time and place, to friend and foe alike, that the torch has been passed to a new _____ of Americans — born in this century, tempered by war, disciplined by a hard and bitter peace, proud of our ancient heritage — and unwilling to witness or permit the slow undoing of those human rights to which this nation has always been committed"

7. Religion became a controversial issue during the presidential campaign. Some feared that John F. Kennedy's allegiance would be to the pope, and not the United States. Speaking to this, he said, "I am not the Catholic candidate for president. I am the _____ Party's candidate for president, who happens also to be a Catholic"

9. President Kennedy identified the common enemies of man as "tyranny, poverty, disease, and _____ itself"

11. President Kennedy's education program faltered because of the issue of _____ aid to parochial schools

13. Governors in nine Appalachian states persuaded President Kennedy to initiate a program to reduce _____ in the mountainous parts of their states

14. As part of a political dynasty that was bringing change to

JOHN F. KENNEDY PRESIDENTIAL LIBRARY & MUSEUM, BOSTON

the country with charisma and strength, some compared President Kennedy to the legendary King Arthur, and his administration to Arthur's _____

15. To counter a recession, President Kennedy sought to _____ taxes

DOWN

2. Congress derailed JFK's plans for a _____ care program for the elderly

3. In his acceptance speech for the presidential nomination, John F. Kennedy stated that Americans were "on the edge of a new _____"

6. At age 43, John F. Kennedy was the _____ man to be elected president

7. President Kennedy was assassinated on November 22, 1963, while visiting this Texas city. Killed barely 1,000 days into his first term, he was unable to complete many of the goals he set out to accomplish

8. John F. Kennedy, the first president of Irish descent, was also the first president born in which century

10. Chose Texan Lyndon B. Johnson, formerly a political opponent, as his _____ president

12. In January 1962, President Kennedy's _____ rating was 77 percent

JOHN F. KENNEDY PRESIDENTIAL LIBRARY & MUSEUM, BOSTON

The Cold War

ACROSS

3. Nikita _____ was the premier of the Soviet Union

6. The United States was in a _____ arms race with the Soviet Union

7. The new government in Cuba, led by Fidel _____, was heavily dependent on the Soviet Union

8. The Limited Nuclear Test _____ Treaty was signed in 1963

10. The Soviet Union built the Berlin _____ to separate East and West Berlin

12. In 1962, the Soviet Union supplied Cuba with nuclear _____. President Kennedy responded with a naval blockade around Cuba, which helped lead to the missile removal

15. The Bay of _____ invasion was a failed attempt at overthrowing the Cuban regime

16. The United States joined the North Atlantic _____ Organization (NATO), a peacekeeping alliance, in 1949

17. The Truman _____ of 1947 promised aid to countries facing communist threats

DOWN

1. Starting in the 1950s, the United States provided military support to _____ Vietnam, sending many U.S. military advisers to train their Army

2. After North Korea invaded South Korea, communist _____ aided the North

4. In 1963, a direct telephone line between Washington and _____, called the "Hotline," was established to improve communications and avoid war

5. The post-World War II _____ Plan authorized economic support to stabilize democratic countries facing communist takeover

9. Before the Cold War, the United States and Soviet Union were _____ during World War II

11. As the Cold War escalated, President Kennedy increased U.S. naval power. The Soviet Union responded by resuming nuclear _____

13. The Soviet Union established communist regimes throughout _____ Europe

14. The Cold War has been defined as a struggle between communism and the _____ market system

JOHN F. KENNEDY PRESIDENTIAL LIBRARY & MUSEUM, BOSTON

Cuban Missile Crisis

ACROSS

2. The Soviet Union had been building a _____ missile base in Cuba, 90 miles from Florida

4. President Kennedy returned early from a trip campaigning for congressional candidates in Chicago to meet with his advisers. To avoid alarming the public, he and his doctor said the president came down with a _____ that required the sudden return

6. President Kennedy met daily with his closest advisers, who served as an Executive Committee of the National _____ Council

7. As part of the resolution, the United States agreed to do away with several air and missile bases in this Middle Eastern country

8. The Soviets agreed to _____ the missiles after the United States agreed not to invade Cuba

10. In aerial photographs of Cuba, Central _____ Agency analysts saw that a missile base was under construction

11. Andrei Gromyko, Soviet _____ minister, assured President Kennedy that the Soviet presence in Cuba was not a threat to the United States

12. McGeorge Bundy, the _____ security adviser, alerted the president to the potential crisis

JOHN F. KENNEDY PRESIDENTIAL LIBRARY & MUSEUM, BOSTON

13. The Cuban Missile Crisis lasted _____ days

15. _____ Castro, brother of Fidel who then led Cuba, visited Moscow in July 1962, strengthening Soviet-Cuban ties

17. President Kennedy ordered a _____ blockade around the Caribbean island nation to disrupt the building of missile bases there

DOWN

1. A spy plane was shot down over Cuba on October 27, 1962 prompting Attorney _____ Robert Kennedy to meet with the Soviet ambassador, who said the plane was violating Cuban air space

3. President Kennedy briefed former Presidents Herbert _____, Harry Truman, and Dwight D. Eisenhower on the crisis

5. On October 26, Cuban Premier Fidel Castro wrote to Soviet leader Nikita Khrushchev urging him to initiate a nuclear first _____ if the United States invaded Cuba

9. On October 22, 1962, President Kennedy gave a _____ address to the nation concerning the crisis

11. United States troops were sent to this state in preparation for an invasion of Cuba

14. Forty thousand Soviet troops, known as the _____ Army, arrived in Cuba undetected by the United States

16. In a letter to Soviet leader Nikita Khrushchev, President Kennedy wrote, "I have not assumed that you or any other sane man would, in this nuclear age, deliberately plunge the world into _____ which it is crystal clear no country could win and which could only result in catastrophic consequences to the whole world, including the aggressor"

Jacqueline Kennedy

ACROSS

3. Born Jacqueline Lee Bouvier in 1929 in this state (two words)

4. Joined her husband on trips, traveling throughout Europe, including the _____ Kingdom, as well as parts of Asia and Latin America

6. Met John F. Kennedy, then a United States senator, while working as the "Inquiring Camera Girl" for the _____ Times-Herald

8. After her husband's death, she worked on creating the John F. Kennedy Presidential _____

9. She died in 1994 and was buried next to the president in _____ National Cemetery

10. Established the White House _____ Association, which published the first official guidebook to the president's home

11. Won a writing competition held by this magazine in 1950

13. The Kennedys' first child

15. Her elegance, grace, and taste made her an icon of the _____ world

ROBERT KNUDSEN, WHITE HOUSE/JOHN F. KENNEDY PRESIDENTIAL LIBRARY & MUSEUM, BOSTON

16. Established a White House Fine _____ Committee to locate and obtain furniture and objects owned by past presidents

17. After the death of her second husband, she started a career in _____

18. Wrote a column called "Campaign _____" while her husband was campaigning for president

DOWN

1. Advocated for the restoration of _____ Avenue, the street connecting the White House and the Capitol

2. Supported the need for a national cultural complex, now the Kennedy Center for the _____ Arts

5. The Resolute Desk, a gift from Queen Victoria in 1878, was restored and placed in the _____ Office

7. Attended Vassar College before studying at the Sorbonne in this French city

12. Married Greek millionaire Aristotle _____ in 1968

13. Her husband dedicated his Pulitzer Prize-winning book, "Profiles in _____," to her

14. Awarded with an honorary _____ Award for her 1962 televised tour of the White House. Millions of viewers tuned in to watch the first lady

The Race to Space

ACROSS

1. Before astronauts were sent to space, _____ were, including monkeys, chimps, and dogs

5. Mission Control is based at NASA's Manned Spacecraft Center — now Johnson Space Center — in this Texas city

9. In 1961, President Kennedy set a goal to land a man on the _____ by the end of the decade

10. Intercontinental _____ missiles (ICBM), which could travel five times faster than the speed of sound, appeared to be the "ultimate weapon"

11. One goal of NASA was to develop _____ that could launch small satellites and probes into space

13. On February 20, 1962, John _____ became the first American to orbit Earth

14. United States _____ satellites were used for reconnaissance to gather information about Soviet activities

16. The Friendship 7 capsule was launched from Cape Canaveral in this state and reached an altitude of 162 miles

18. Neil Armstrong walked on the moon in 1969. He famously stated, "That's one small step for man, one giant leap for _____"

DOWN

1. Created in 1958, NASA stands for National _____ and Space Administration

2. The _____ Program was created to land people on the moon

3. President Kennedy appointed Vice President Lyndon B. _____ to head the National Aeronautics and Space Council

JOHN F. KENNEDY PRESIDENTIAL LIBRARY & MUSEUM, BOSTON

4. Members of the Russian space program are known as _____

6. President Kennedy marketed the space race as a competition between communism and _____

7. Soviet Valentina Tereshkova became the first _____ cosmonaut in space in 1963

8. In 1959, during the presidency of Dwight D. _____ seven men became astronauts for Project Mercury

12. The Soviet Union launched the satellite _____ in 1957, prompting fears that the technology meant missiles with nuclear warheads launched in Europe could reach the United States

13. The goal of Project _____ was to perfect the re-entry maneuvers of spacecraft

15. Project Mercury's goal was to orbit the _____ in a manned spacecraft

17. President Kennedy said, "We have a long way to go in the space race. We started late. But this is the new ocean, and I believe the United States must sail on it and be in a position second to _____"

Vietnam

ACROSS

1. In 1954, the _____ Accords divided Vietnam into communist North and non-communist South

6. Some Buddhist _____ set themselves on fire during protests

8. Henry Cabot Lodge served as the United States _____ to South Vietnam

11. Speaking of Vietnam, President Kennedy said in 1963, "In the final analysis, it is their war. They are the ones who have to win it or lose it. We can help them, we can give them equipment, we can send our men out there as advisers, but they have to win it, the people of Vietnam, against the _____... But I don't agree with those who say we should withdraw. That would be a great mistake"

13. While president, Lyndon B. _____ authorized American combat troops to participate in military action

15. The North sent _____ forces into the South in hopes of conquering it

16. North Vietnam used the Ho Chi Minh _____, a network of roads from North Vietnam to South Vietnam by way of Laos and Cambodia, to aid the North Vietnamese Army and Vietcong

DOWN

1. The United States eventually supported the overthrow of the South Vietnamese _____

2. Formerly French-controlled Indochina was made up of three countries: Vietnam, Laos, and _____

3. The Vietnam War ended during the presidency of Richard _____

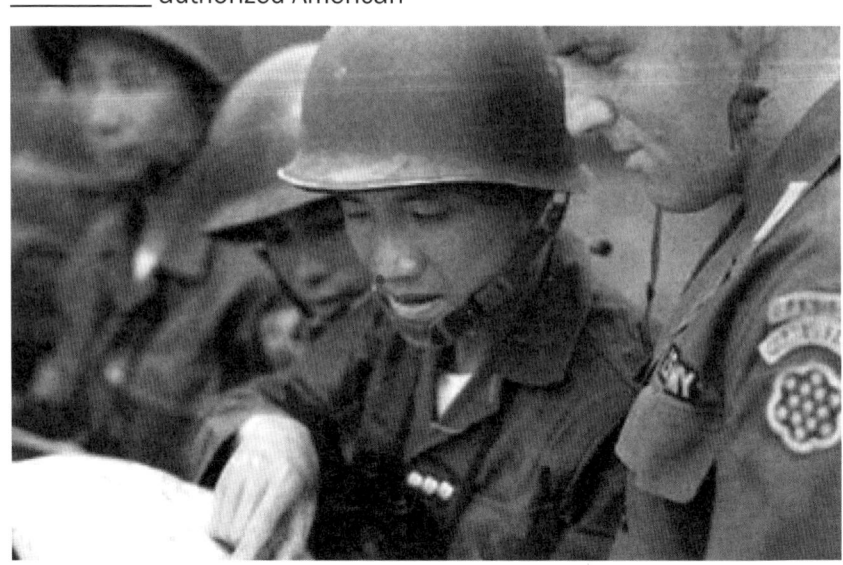

U.S. ARMY CENTER OF MILITARY HISTORY

4. The National _____ Front was a political organization aimed at overthrowing the South Vietnamese government and reuniting the North and South

5. The _____ theory was based on the belief that if one country fell to communism, others would follow

7. Though a formal agreement ending the conflict was reached in 1973, North Vietnam invaded and captured _____, South Vietnam's capital, in 1975, leading to the evacuation of all the remaining Americans from the embassy

9. After President Kennedy took office, he sent more _____ advisers and aid to South Vietnam

10. In 1955, the Southeast _____ Treaty Organization was formed to prevent communist expansion

11. In November 1963, weeks before President Kennedy's assassination, a military _____ took place in South Vietnam

12. South Vietnam suppressed Buddhist religious leaders and followers, destroying their temples and instituting _____ law, leading to the Buddhist crisis

14. From 1955 to 1963, South Vietnam's leader was Ngo Dinh _____

JOHN F. KENNEDY PRESIDENTIAL LIBRARY & MUSEUM, BOSTON

Civil Rights and John F. Kennedy

ACROSS

4. John F. Kennedy helped secure the release of the Reverend Martin Luther King Jr. from jail in 1960, and won more than 70 percent of the black vote in his _____ victory

5. After some freedom riders were attacked, _____ Kennedy urged Congress to desegregate interstate transportation and ensure safety

6. President Kennedy sent National Guardsmen to the University of Mississippi to ensure that James _____, a black man, could register for classes

7. The National Association for the _____ of Colored People (NAACP) was founded in 1909

9. The separation of the races is known as _____

12. Martin Luther King Jr. called this Alabama city the most segregated in the country. His 1963 sit-ins, protests, and marches led to mass arrests. President Kennedy sent thousands of troops to the state to diffuse the violence

13. President Kennedy placed Vice President Johnson in charge of the President's Committee on Equal _____ Opportunity

14. The Reverend Martin Luther King Jr. gave his famous "I Have a _____" speech during the 1963 March on Washington which celebrated the centennial of the Emancipation Proclamation

15. The Civil Rights Act, which did not pass until after President Kennedy's assassination, enforced the desegregation of _____

DOWN

1. Alabama Governor George _____ believed in "segregation now, segregation tomorrow, and segregation forever." In 1963, he physically stood in the way of two black students trying to enroll at the state university. President Kennedy responded by addressing the nation and announcing civil rights legislation

2. The Civil Rights Act outlawed racial _____ in public accommodations such as hotels, restaurants, and theatres

3. The Civil Rights Act authorized the withdrawal of _____ funds from programs practicing discrimination

5. President Kennedy appointed an unprecedented number of blacks to high-level positions in the administration and strengthened the Civil _____ Commission

8. _____ rights was a main focus of Attorney General Robert Kennedy, as he worked to guarantee suffrage to African Americans

10. In 1961, the Congress of _____ Equality organized "Freedom Rides" to desegregate transportation

11. The Civil Rights Act granted blacks protection at election _____

History of the Peace Corps

ACROSS

2. A Peace Corps volunteer serves for _____ years

5. Some Peace Corps returnees have been elected to _____, including Senators Paul Tsongas and Christopher Dodd

7. An _____ order in 1961 established the Peace Corps

9. On October 14, 1960, then-Senator John F. Kennedy spoke at the University of _____ in Ann Arbor, challenging students to live and work in developing countries

10. In his inaugural address, President Kennedy said, "To those people in the huts and villages of half the globe struggling to break the bonds of mass misery, we pledge our best efforts to help them help _____"

12. President Kennedy hoped the Peace Corps would help spread _____ to other countries

13. In 1971, President Richard _____ put foreign and domestic volunteer programs, including the Peace Corps, into a new agency called ACTION. Later, President Jimmy Carter restored Peace Corps' independence

14. In the late 1990s, President Bill _____ pushed and got more funding to expand Peace Corps programs

15. In the 1980s, President Ronald Reagan expanded Peace Corps programs to include _____ literacy and business-related education

DOWN

1. The Peace Corps has been popular with _____ graduates throughout its history

3. In its history, the Peace Corps has had more than 200,000 _____ working in 139 countries

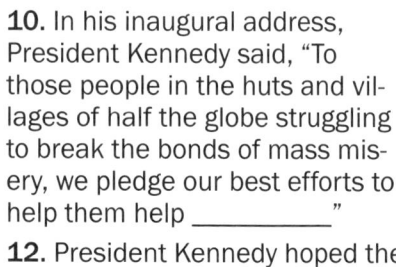

JOHN F. KENNEDY PRESIDENTIAL LIBRARY & MUSEUM, BOSTON

4. Crisis Corps, created in 1995 as part of the Peace Corps, provides short term assistance after natural disasters abroad and at home, such as Hurricane _____ in 2005

6. In 2002, Habitat for _____ and the Peace Corps began working on projects together

8. In 1989, Hungary became the first _____ European country to have a Peace Corps program

11. After the _____ War, volunteer numbers declined and funding for the Peace Corps was cut

13. In 1985, a program offered training for returned volunteers to become teachers in _____ _____ City

JOHN F. KENNEDY PRESIDENTIAL LIBRARY & MUSEUM, BOSTON

Before the Presidency

The Kennedy Dynasty

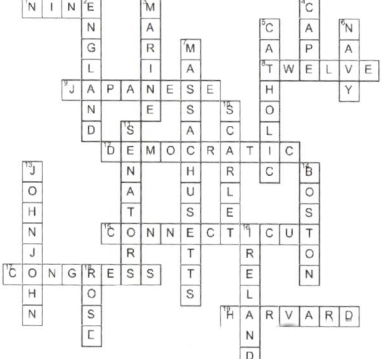

WWII and John F. Kennedy

America During the Early 1960s

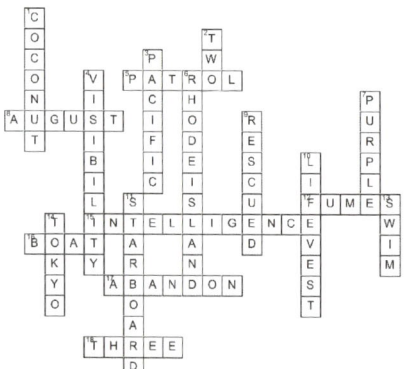

The 35th President of the United States

The Cold War

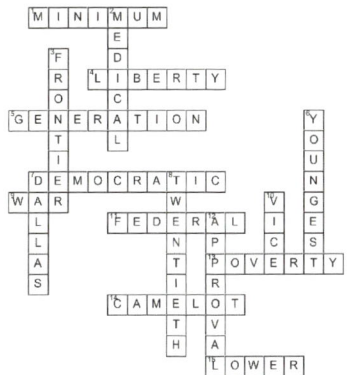

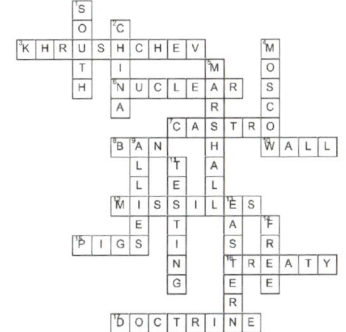

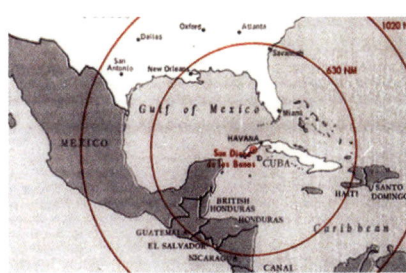
Cuban Missile Crisis

Jacqueline Kennedy

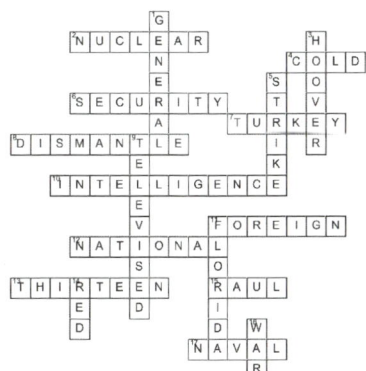

Vietnam

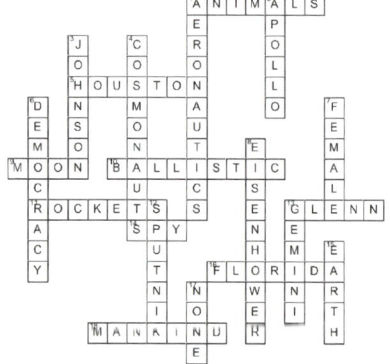
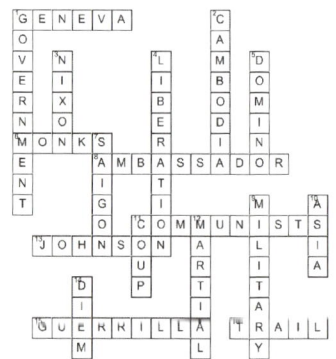

Civil Rights and John F. Kennedy

History of the Peace Corps

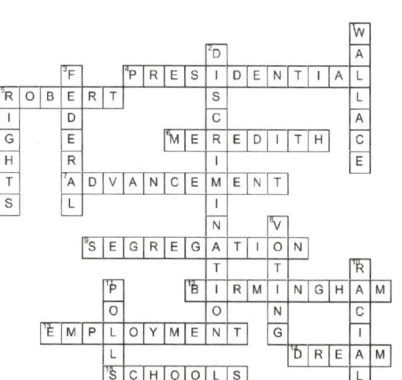
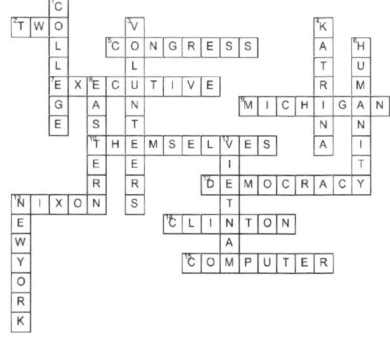